Drunk Poets

Ben Bachand and Janna Christen

DEDICATION

To all of those who have come and gone and are currently in our lives; your love, passions and insight have inspired us and, even if only in memory, will continue to do so for the rest of our lives.

❖

You have to be always drunk. That's all there is to it--it's the only way. So as not to feel the horrible burden of time that breaks your back and bends you to the earth, you have to be continually drunk. But on what? Wine, poetry or virtue as you wish. But be drunk. And if sometimes, on the steps of a palace or the green grass of a ditch, in the mournful solitude of your room, you wake again, drunkenness already diminishing or gone, ask the wind, the wave, the star, the bird, the clock, everything that is flying, everything that is groaning, everything that is rolling, everything that is singing, everything that is speaking...ask what time it is and wind, wave, star, bird, clock will answer you: "It is time to be drunk! So as not to be the martyred slaves of time, be drunk, be continually drunk! On wine, on poetry or on virtue as you wish."
~ Charles Baudelaire ~
❖

A BIT ABOUT THE BOOK

This ad-hoc collection of poems is more like a series of journal entries and our poetic styles are very different; we hope you find something, at least one poem, to connect with.

The poetry by Ben has numbers based on a personal system of organization. The 'RO' and 'lo' endings designate a particular person the poem is written about. 'EBE' was intended as part of a series in which the End is the Beginning is the End, title and last word being interchangeable.

The poetry by Janna, though inspired by many individuals and different life experiences, is not quite as efficiently organized. Such a broad variety of influences tend to blend together in her work, along with her own imagination and artistic interpretation, that her resulting poetry is simply a moment to be experienced and interpreted through the readers own lens.

Mantra 1

Set yourself limits made for breaking,
and a way of life meant to followed.

Build a code of you,
represent all that you want to be.

Realize what all you are.

See your flaws
and don't hate yourself when they aren't fixed
overnight.

See your strengths and celebrate,
quietly.

Enjoy your life,
and laugh loudly.

047-b

I sit here and type because I want you to
understand
my time here
my relationships
how I feel.

My hopes
and how I've failed.

I want you to know
I love you,
        whoever you are
        however you are.

We have shared something
and I am grateful for it.

(Keep Listening)

073-b

Every second I'm with you,
      is another I don't have to wish I was.

-lo

Blueprints

Blue eyes look into blue eyes
And reflected in pools of blue
I see a future with you.

And caught in the corner of your smile
And in the tuck of your ribs
The blueprint of our home lives

Measurements will be made in your hands
widths
And counters will be level at my hips
So that when we kiss in the kitchen
And you lift my legs to wrap around your waist
Our home will be made in detail-
Expecting that embrace.

Glass (Holding On)

You are the feeling
of when my hand fits perfectly
around that last glass of wine before bed,

You are the nook my thumb finds
in the handle of my coffee cup.

and You are the nervousness that my fingers
tap on the table top
when I have no cup to hold.

but when my hands are near yours
and they fit perfectly
and my thumb finds that nook in yours
there is no nervousness,

I am content.

Time Keepers

Your weight is welcome.
The tone of your body is vibrating in my bones
Your toes curling into the souls of my feet
Trying to get some grasp on this sacred ground.

Our waists meet in metronome.
Two hourglass time keepers
Measuring out the moments
    The minutes
        The seconds
            The movements.

Our collarbones wink at each other
Tricks of light and sweat saying more than our
breath allows.

Hands grasping hands
Grasping hair
Hugging shoulder blades
Fingers digging into the halfmoons
Where wings would be

And we are flying anyways
Until we hit the ceiling of our physical reality
And for a moment cease to be –
Broken and shattered into more space than a
body can take up.

We take our time putting the pieces back
together.

174-b

[Whisper This]

Say it slow...   (behind the ear)

Whisss
      per

the breathy 'h' feels like an ache
a subtle 's' at the edge of the tongue, dry
the perfect 'per' needs wetted lips
a short release of damp breath
      per
          fect   -ly shaped

little bumps on the back of your neck

Art

Fingertips trace
Hands around a waist-
Lingering on a hipbone
Rush of breath cut smooth by moan

Names said like prayers
Hanging in the air
Mixing with salt damp
Body by body
An eternity of touch constant

Lips part
To let slip a piece of heart
Perfect curve back arch

Moments where we achieve Art

077-b

I love all the pieces of you
      all the pieces I can't pick up
      all the pieces I've scattered
      all the pieces I'll never see again

I love you and I hate myself
      for what I've done
      for what I can't do
      for what I can't give you

All of the memories I can't save
      they pass slowly through my fingers
      they pass slowly from my mind
pieces of my heart
      and who I am
grains of my soul

How could I have ever told you
I was not in love with you?

I've loved you since the moment I met you
and will until the moment I die.

-RO

143-b

I feel as if I had just woke from a troubled
sleep;

where I had missed you for a time longer than I
can remember.

-lo

Brail

Hips kiss
And thighs slide by

Arms loop my waist so tight,
Your fingers
        slowly
           replace
              my
                  ribs
And your thumbs become my spine

I am breathing into your palms
  -I swear my lungs are breathing for us both...

Collarbones become bites
And shoulders [blinders]
As I sink into a world that doesn't need sight.

Forgive me if I left a mark-
It will be my brail in the morning
To remember what we were
If things don't wake up right.

151-b

My tired eyes
look out
at our tired lives

sad because
we don't feel the same

years gone by
and I
see through our lies

to a life
with too much blame

but I don't mind
holding-on too long

because our love
will always be the same.

-RO

Trace

Our histories were written in the eyes of others
Before we understood what it was we had seen.

Our futures were forecasted
By the smiles of family
And the tension of fingertips when you touched
     me.

You read my heartline in the third person
But didn't give me your name,
Shook my hand
And walked away.

082-b

Lipstick Tells

I couldn't read her lips
or remember what she'd said
about the different shades of red.

-lo

180-b

I thought us close
but close, my dear,
is no where near enough

it's likely we
thought love to be
much stronger and stranger stuff

Black and White and Whiskey

His smile is practiced and his words are always
thought out beforehand.
Unless he's been drinking whiskey,
And then his personal truths tumble out.
The truths that no one wants others to know,
The same ones he thinks he keeps so well
       hidden.
It's not a shock though,
Because you can see Him between the polished
       periods
Of his sober oh-so-structured-sentences,
And that's what makes him human.

He lives in a world of black and whites.
Which seems like it would be uncomfortable.
But perhaps the rigid outlines give him support,
So that he can succeed in all the ways he thinks
       he's supposed to.
It seems to be working for him,
You can see it in the eyes of others.
Respect is something that he will never be at a
loss for.

He's worried that I will run away from him,
To discover myself and travel the world.
I want to tell him to run with me,
To be part of my adventure and discovery.
But the world's not exactly black and white,

And when your crossing that many borders,
Something as delicate as personal lines tend to
    sway.

49mg

Tinted lips draw me in
Your red wine kisses crusted
With late night conversations

Lips that swallow pills
Lips that touch other lips
Lips that are numb to the difference of lies and
      truths
Lips that are delicate in their abuse
So subtle in their use
That you would never know they were feeding
      you poison

Your taste is tinted with hemlock
The flavor of you is shaded cyanide
And though I know I am killing myself slowly,
That are no other lips I'd rather die by.

092-b

Shots

Liquid emotion
you pour and I drink a fire
burning up and down

Glass (Broken)

The last sip of wine
And I know I drank too much tonight

You told me an hour ago
      - with your eyes -
That it wasn't going to be sweet dreams
That after everyone left -
    Our party wasn't going to end.

You think I didn't hear when you punched a
hole in our bathroom wall
And I told everyone
    Everything was all right

I drank too much tonight
But now that's the only time we talk
    -Eyes or otherwise-

128-b

It's you who brings me down
and the world around my ears

Flightless

He had a thing for girls with broken wings.
Take them in and whisper words
That float like ravens on the wind…
Dark and fleeting
Ready to sweep you up,
And so graceful…
That every time you thought you were falling
It was just another dip in his dance.

He had a thing for girls with broken wings.
He said that they had seen more of life-
That they had flown too high, or too far, or with
too much fight.
And now they need a place-
A cage with an open door.

But if he has a things for girls with broken
wings,
Then what was it that he saw broken in me
When I thought that it was I
That had found him flightless…

(Wo)Man Overboard

In the current of conversation,
We had reached rapids.

That moment when words are confused with
      froth
And people shout adrenaline sourced thoughts
Virtues and motivations and beliefs about the
      world
Try desperately to anchor safe eddies of calm
And the want to know the depth of the person
      next to you
Becomes a necessity
We all know hope floats
But a flood is coming
And I need something more tangible to hold on
      to

As our waters were rising
And I looked to you for security
I realized that this life preserver I had built
      from my image of you
Was slowly being filled with pebbles of doubt
      and negative reality.

Your thought were only a stone throw away
      from mine
But were just enough off shore to sink.
And slowly this weight

Of your stone shaped thoughts
Have been pulling down the life raft I had
        constructed.

It was foolish of me to think you'd be a strong
        enough swimmer to save two.
When it's not a life or death situation,
It's everyman for himself –
Women and children first doesn't apply.

Abandon ship.

I should have thought more about keeping my
        head above water
Than just treading water and waiting for you.

Our Digital Romance

You're right there, on the other side of a digital
    romance.
It's as if our thoughts translate perfectly into
    binary code
And are reassembled on the other side with a
    common aesthetic-
Where we find beauty and perfection in
    conversations without a face.

Too many times our words have remembered a
    love
That our bodies in combination seem to have
    forgotten.
And the memories are so good,
That lessons learned become white noise on a
    collect call
That at the time we are more than willing to pay
    the price for.

A withdrawal of a few cents from the emotional
    bank..
Though with our history it's apparent that
common sense isn't included in the cost.

Our voices from years of experience know how
    to whisper and woo,
And the tension is so great that sometimes I'm
    afraid the letters of my words will break

If I answer too quickly.

I wonder, after all the wooing is done, and our
        words aren't padded by distance,
When your head is on the pillow next to mine,
Rather than thousands of miles away,
Will we continue to be so kind?

Has a digital romance given us a protection
        from verbal daggers that can only be
        thrown close range?
We have left each other in bruises and tears
        before.
And time and again rediscover a love that ends
        with just as much sorrow as it started.

It could be different this time.
And what if it is?
What ifs are only ever so far away.
But maybe it's this distance that makes it
possible.

What if our "what if" is the vanishing point of
        hopelessly in love.
Always in view but impossible to reach...
Except through this extension
Our Digital Romance.

Copper Pennies

It tastes a bit like copper pennies
Which surprisingly taste a bit like blood.
       - Don't ask me how I know these
             things...
(Though the latter most often comes from
       biting my tongue
after I realize I've said too much
when really I had nothing to say at all.)

It tastes like copper pennies-
A sweet metallic tingle
That leaves the insides of your cheeks aching
And wondering a half hour after you spit it out
What that flavor was...

The more favorable but similar situation of this
Is when you've found that perfect something
That hit the spot for your cravings
And after a while, when you want it again
You have to remember
What it was that you ate.

That favorable but similar situation is love.
Copper pennies are heart break.

Which is why I laugh sometimes
When they say change is good for you.

050-b

The days go bye,
slowly and quickly sometimes
with more weight than the numbers
representing them,
      the months hurt
      and the years might kill me
I miss you in numbers
and more than that,
I can no longer stand to think about.

095-b

Falling Leaves

Does it hurt
     for me to watch

you undress so carelessly
     whichever way the wind seems to blow

No

I know it necessary
     for you to let go

-RO

052-b

It's not just a physical connection
or being "in-love"

It's being intoxicated by the mere presence
and afterward the lingering

addiction

I'm not, 'Afraid
that I may never find something like this again.'
I know.
I never will.

I think of my wife
and how she's married to another man.

-RO

172-b

If I should not see or speak to you again,
know that I,
     with all my heart and life, my love,
      had meant to.

Goodbye for now, my dear, I love you.

-RO

Screw No Longer

I thought that all my threads had been worn
I could no longer make that connection

       That close fit – The ability to take hold –
And stay…

A fastening that lasts and maintains
Under presser and tension,
That will matter-of-factly be tested.

But when your connection turns to grip
       And your grip turns to bite
              And when that bite begins to
                    rust….
There is no doubt of infection.

Even a girl made of iron
Falls to frailty
       When too much   empty space
             Is let in
And all her sharp edges fade….

Here - with all my threads worn
   My ego smoothed
And my passions streamlined
I doubted my ability to find a depth that would
hold

But then I met a carpenters son
And I learned that a screw with no bite

Is simply a nail

And nails are far easier to build with.

150-b

Then one day
when I was done
        searching for adventure
I found myself at home

and it was exactly where I wanted to be.

116-b

a creative commotion
a cacophony of action in our kitchen
a painter and portrait maker
making more of life in minutes
than many match in years
and ears open to the spoken word
of poets and musicians
sitting on the floor
and coming and going
in and out of doors
the cooking smoke hangs in the air
some in the eyes
most in parted lips and smiles.

the tea potted
and trivets ill used
a house a home
warm and worn
by the use of many bodies
turned into lives

127-b

Seeping through the daily news
colors an editor would never use
a stained table
an artist
who can part us
pen and paper
brush and stroke

      another canvas
      another time
      another idea

painted together
shown apart

it takes more than time
to sketch
an artists heart

Cherries

I was always the excited one
Who saw the fresh fruit at the farmers market
And brought far too much home.

It was a good idea –
And we would laugh and snack,
And feed each other peaches and cherries
Until our stomachs hurt.

And in the fridge the other 9 baskets
Of my over abundant wealth would sit
And gain spots of imperfection

Softness and a few bad bruises,
Signs of time passing always leave a mark.
But you were never one to let that bad apple
spoil the bunch.

You were the one
Who would take my forgotten fruit,
Carve out the divots and the dents,
Coat them with sugar and cream
And remind me after supper
Of our everyday delights.

075-b

A cold night
with a breeze
we walk
and my friends talk
into the wind

I raise my glass
to the stars
and they laugh
and drunkenly fall
to spin round

as they had done
since we and mankind
were children.

137-b

Memories

Planes and open doors
      to nowhere
      no one special

full of longing and wishing
      we were
      all somewhere else

above the clouds
      the world
      a dream

we land in what we create
      sometimes new
      memories

-EBE

157-b

My friend on stage
singing his words
making a living sound
so easy

If Our Lives Lasted Longer Than Concrete

Dashboard lights across your face
Highlighting the worry on your browline,
Tucked in the corners of your mouth...
A yellow-green glow trying to fake moonlight
Dirty with memories and melancholy-
The color of something left outside too long.

The turn signal becomes a warning light.
A morass code SOS signaling the turn to a
driveway

Where we sit

The tension between us is like the space
        between branches
Connected despite the grey-sky distance
But somehow unable to reach back to our roots.

Maybe if we sit here long enough,
The rubber tires will erode,
The metal under our feet will corrode and wear
        away.
Moss and mushrooms,
Fungus and ferns will creep in-
And maybe the softness of a neutral nature will
        oxidize our hardened exteriors.

Once the pavement is gone,

Maybe then our ruts will be also...
And without the deadest intention of forward
        movement
Perhaps we can look around and take a moment
        to breath.

Distracted from our concentrated concerns
Once held pressure tight with rolled up
        windows
The fresh air might put power in our lungs
And we cough out those conversations
        tarnished with rust and too much time
        kept in.

Open air will diffuse the lead heavy lyrics
And we can walk on,
Natural light bounding off our shoulders.

087-b

What I Must Write

He's not coming back
he burned the box of you
        and your things
        his memories

alight with a passion
that is undeniably his future
        without you
        apart from you.

How can he hold any of us
as close as he once held you?

so do not torment us
with words like 'respect' and 'friendship'
when love and desire
are ablaze

Critic

The tingle of you down my spine
Is a song I connected to long ago,
Now assigned to a memory that has become
bittersweet and abstract
A watercolor seismograph
Painted in the era of realism –
Remembered by a post modern mind.

The tingle of you down my spine
Is a tattoo that ricochets off my vertebra
Leaving stray geometric shapes between my ribs
    Making perfectly symmetrical sense –
      With a chaos that compliments our
      history.

The tingle of you is art.

You have left a mark on me.
Like cracks in Japanese pottery-
You have filled in some weak spaces with gold
And celebrated my imperfection.

But art is in the eye of the beholder –
And with hindsight being 20/20
Things are bound to look different now.

Once More

I'm addicted to you and this is my relapse.
We lost our cloths before bars his last call-
Between heavy breathing, we find laughter,
We are caught in this moment, all limbs and
      sprawl.

A jawline mellow and relaxed-
We unplugged the light from the wall
The order of sheets doesn't matter
We are lost in the tangle of it all.

Our body's carry out movements that are more
      than acts
We trust a feeling that's more than emotional
      recall
This bliss isn't just physical, it's a moment
      sought after
We are playing with fire, and it's a drug that's
      lethal.

178-b

Who knew it'd be harder,
     writing in the darkness?

With all the lights on
     except the one within me

The Misfits

I am made of tidbits of character
The 80's black leather rocker
And the highschool choir girl.

My attitudes are misfits
Ranging from Zen lecturer
To helter skelter
To "Who let that bitch in?
          And why'd they keep her?"

My kicks come in various sizes...
Keds at the farmers market
Heels that scream fuck it
And barefoot so I can see a little of my soul
          When I can't remember where I hid it...

I read the Kama Sutra
And wonder why its not still an art
I read Kafka
Get pissed at the judge,
And wonder why only a cockroach seems to do
his part
I read Cosmo
And wonder if I'm pear shaped, or apple...
          ...or just a tart.

I try to find a definition
That I can lay myself under

To protect myself from mental and verbal
thunder...

But I see myself in others,
And recognize that rarely can one word provide
a cover...
All I can say is,
Don't judge her.

A(r)mor

I don't need more broken hearts to wear on my
sleeve
The weight of that much oxidized love turns a
rusty brown
And drags you down like the metal armor it's
become.

Gauntlets and greaves aren't becoming on one
so young.
But it helps to keep your knuckles from being
scraped and your shins from being torn
When you manage to crawl away from the last
battle lost.

I am a damsel in distress
And I am tired of rescuing myself.

053-b

A flower cut
may yet serve as decoration
if it chooses not to die

but

it will still rot.

141-b

~~MANIC~~

Obsession is like living with a disease you enjoy
too much,
you just want to keep treating it
and in the end, you hope it kills you.

041-b

The Grave

I drive with only the vaguest idea
of where the road goes
. . .
knowing it to be
a concrete destination.

071-b

We can't get back
all the things we think we lost
they were never ours

Stranger

The restless feeling that hits you at 4am.
It hits you so hard, that sometimes it wakes you
up.
But sometimes it just hangs out and whispers,
Making you think you forgot something.

And sometimes you try so hard to remember
what it is that you forgot
That for a moment you forget how to love the
person sleeping next to you.
And for a moment, you're in bed with a
stranger,
And you're listening to their breath,
Wondering how well they know you,
And if they ever get late night amnesia too.

066-b

Some lives pass
        like the comings and goings of the wind

but unexpected tears dry quickly

089-b
Survivors

We are the lucky ones

the perpetrators and the victims

the soldiers
      who marched in a hundred years of war
          every hero
               and their vanquish

we are every measure
      and its mete

Our desires compass the world, we
      -Conquerors-
        have fought for and to defend
           each point.

We are the monarchs and the kings
      the successes
         and their successors

We are the whores and drunks
      the failures
         and their jailors

We have lived a thousand lives
        we are the generations and iterations
           of all other mortal men

to every scheme within the minds of them
          we are privy

We have seen the sun set and rise
        each day
        a billion times
        through twice as many eyes

We flee
We fight
We conquer

The World

Our inheritance, earned,

        has no better place
           than in the hearts
                    minds
                       and
hands
        of us...
           ...survivors,
               let us dream and act
        not as we are but as one,
immortal species
                           GODS

Crushed

Beneath the feet of Gods – crushed.

Cast in shadows we can never live up too –
Standards created in our collective mind.

I'd like to think that Gods are created in
perfection,
Because to error is human…
And we need something better than flaw to
look up to –
An impossible standard to keep us in line.

Perhaps that is what drives us to drink –
That in our reliance on communion,
And from the comfort of the blood of Christ –
We seek to absolve our souls
From the guilt built in the form of idols.

165-b

I only write
     what I think is right
to right the wrongs
     within me

080-b

I shake myself awake
and take stock
burdens and injuries
are not a loss
some memories, remembered
and floating in the breach

a
neat
white
house

who (comma!) would picket about a fence?!
but perhaps a front
the store
out of white
paint
ed faces
and the mask I'll have to wear today
everyday
a mockery of self
and ideas
held-in
like a breath
of what might have been
          reality in
the moment of a dream.

Atlas

There is a warmth in your eyes
And you have been built with strong arms and a
    broad chest-
Ready to hold someone's world up if you
    needed to.
But your words come from textbooks and
    study...
And the organic nature that all relationships
    should grow out of
Has been tinted with your self-help fertilizer.
An unnatural brightness glows in your train of
    thought,
And lectures and comforts grow side by side in
    a garden that's been too well tended.

I ache for those empty stretches of emotional
    fields.
The ones that are dotted with pools and
    wildflowers,
All genuine, and worth so much more for the
    wind they stand up against.
I want a garden that's been lost to the weeds of
    distractions, new passions, and
    unforeseen interaction.
Because I've found that in these beds, the seeds
    of reality have been planted.
Give me excellent imperfection where
    movement is rejoiced,

The unexpected color and form,
Recognition of a significance that can come
      from unguarded moments.
And all the loss and decay is left out of the
      analyzers microscope
So it can sink into the loamy truths of life
And from this pace of wilderness and
      abandoned method,
We can live in a world that won't need to be
      held up
Because we won't be afraid to fall.

I want a partner with a green thumb,
Not one structured from stone.

He's No North Star

I want to draw constellations between your
shoulder blades.

Your body is a cosmos that I am continually lost
in...
In exploration I discover new galaxies in the
bend of your knees,
Supernovas collected at your collarbone,
And spacejunk caught under your fingernails.

If I could, I would name you my Polaris.
But that name was given away long ago,
And it's too much responsibility for someone
who is perpetually expanding
And hasn't found their center.

Lets Live at the Mountain Tops

The weight of gravity at sea level
Is something we don't notice, our bodies won't
tell us
       About the extra weight
Because we already feel pressed upon
By jobs and relationships and the time limits on
groupon...
The future continues on
But what we think about is the con
Of keeping up with the Jones'

We Jones for the pay raise bonuses
And the bogus promises
Of a happy life after retirement
When we can quit
Working for the weekends
And make commitments
To the passion
That when we were young
We were hellbent on making come true.

But have you been to the mountain tops?
The air up there is inspiring
Invigorating and full of higher meaning –
Energy that is constantly continuing and
expiring.

But our lungs aren't used to the deep breaths

Our bodies aren't used to all engines firing
We are used to being a panicked mess
Of shallow ins and outs and voiceless stress

If only we could rearrange our misplacements
And lighten the load of self contained deadlines
and assignments

Then maybe with our new found buoyancy
We can live at the mountain tops,
Instead of just staring at them.

Wanderlust

The wind of my wanderlust whistles low
And I am left to wonder why my waist
And ribs still expand when my breathing is so
shallow.

We are all wandering, living on one whim
      Or another

Wishes are wasteful when fed on wine.

My Bibles

I strive to be
A person who lives by the sea.
Moving with the ebb and flow –
The new expanse of land at noon
And the ever shrinking world at midnight.
Flux and pull

I strive to be
A person who lives with good words.
I want to weigh and measure the vowels allowed
on my lips –
The strength of a well timed silence

I want my bibles
To be a tidebook and a pocket dictionary –
My new and old testament
Relying on the turning of the world
And the responsibility of the phrase I turn over
time.

When someone sums me up,
I want somehow, for
My respect for what is said -
And my acknowledgment of how some things
can't be,
To be apparent.
How the tides will come and words will go
And all one can do
Is learn best how to deal with them.

061-b

I sit
ink wet
pines scratching at the wind
bent by it
bowing
in respect

Forever and Eternity

These cliffs have been feeding themselves to
the ocean for years,
Sustaining a give and take relationship that we
don't have life times long enough to see.

I sit in the scoop of a sea worn rock
One that has been caressed and hollowed long
before the marriage of this slope and sea.
A dowry gift symbolizing the solidity of their
union.

And I enjoy the length of their engagement.
Long enough to carve out pews of stone for
those that come and go.

No rushing.

Instead they have taken the time to develop
their identities
To define their separations and similarities
So they will never lose the other
To the new identity of a relationship
When two become one   .

I sit only as a spectator to the ceremony
Listening to vows I can't quite translate.
Tumbling in the dialects of birdsong and
wavecrash.

And though I don't know the words
I'd like to think I know what they're saying.

They are saying to each other -
That he doesn't care about the history buried in
her bones
The dust that has settled in her fine lines
Or the marks that other men may have left.

Just as she doesn't mind the other shores he's
explored
The piles of trash and treasure that he's
hoarded
Or the many moments that someone else has
laid in his bed,

Their pasts have lasted for so long
That it would be foolish not to forgive the life
that happens
When you haven't yet found your true love yet
(Even when they have brushed by each other
for years)

They are telling each other
How they will share forever and eternity
Either as slope, or as sea, or the murky in-
between...
It won't matter.

Because together,
They are just as they should be.

049-b

In Vain

the pieces
the messages

skillfully left

beautifully

in many mediums and ways

through time

we try so valiantly
to communicate
one to another

Mission Impossible: This Message Will Not Self Destruct

Be at peace.

Learn to be okay with the fact
That you won't always get to stay there.

Stop looking for the moment when you're done
with this,
And when you'll finally be there.
"here" and "now" are the only places you ever
really exist.

Don't use living in the present as an excuse
For not being aware of your future.

Give in to the truth that you make your own
happiness.
Every moment is influenced by your own
choice.

Give in to the reality that at times you will make
your own torment,
But that that's okay,
Because what you learn from it
Can make it worth it.

Love the little things.
Make them bigger than they may seem.
And love them honestly.

If you don't love it,
Do something else.

Cherish your family.
Create bonds.
Respect yourself.
Empathize with others.

Be at peace....Repeat.

DON'T PANIC